"Travel is the only thing you buy that makes you richer."

59

COFFEE ROASTERS
LOT SIXTY ONE
of
AMSTERDAM
lot sixty one
x
Urban Outfitters

GELDORP

LONDON

GAMBRINUS

DIM
SUM
NOW

't hotel
18
't hotel

146

PLOP

RENTAL
16
THE END IS NIGH

20

The HEART & Hand
UPPER
United ALES

10

AMSTEL

27

P

P

Pieternel

ENGEL & VÖLKERS

RAÏNARAÏ
Bakfiets.nl

Harwoods

32

ADT

CONSULAT

ODETTE

Au Vieux Paris
d'Arcole

LOGEMENTS
CLAUZEL

SAN MARINA

UJD 538S

7

FGP
665J

46

50

ROGUE GALLERY
MONOCLE
NKX 799H

H127
FHG

15

ANSIONS

EERSTE PASSEERDERS
DWARSSTRAAT CENTRUM
62½/m 104
130

177

HEMPSTOR

DL-06-26

BOUNTY
Gili AIR

21

lazy cats.

醬

武家醋坊

BRIGADE · STATION
NKX 799H

27

42-40
40

70
68

AM
70-33

CARLTON MID
ROAD
TRAIN

KOSHER BUTCHERY

NO PARKING

ELEVEN

16

MOYNAT

FGP
665J

16

ST MARKS
ROAD W11

WARREN
MEWS W1

ST LUKES STR

CENTRAL
FIRE STATION

AL-TASNEEM

55$
017 25 25 40
078 335 777
STHENG

ART CENTER NIGHTMA KET

THE ONE

2B-7412

51

PAPIERMOLEN

4
THE ADVENTURE STARTS HERE
401 - 411
412–431

ONLY

BOROUGH OF CHELSEA
DRAYCOTT AVENUE
S.W.3

A426 XFT

patagonia

25

CPSIA information can be obtained
at www.ICGtesting.com
Printed in the USA
BVHW021621300719
554670BV00012B/236/P

9 780464 110200